D1175300

Condoleezza Rice

Precious McKenzie

R urke
Educational Media

rourkeeducationalmedia.com

Teacher Notes available at
rem4teachers.com

© 2013 Rourke Educational Media

All rights reserved. No part of this book may be reproduced or utilized in any form or by any means, electronic or mechanical including photocopying, recording, or by any information storage and retrieval system without permission in writing from the publisher.

www.rourkeeducationalmedia.com

PHOTO CREDITS: Cover, page 13, 16 - 18, 21: © AP Images; title page: © Department of State; page 5a: © LOC/Marion Post Wolcott; page 5b, 6: © LOC/Marion S. Trikosko; page 7: © LOC/Dick MeMarsico; page 8a: © LOC/author unknown; page 8b: red_frog; page 9: © Mike Thomas; page 11: © Wikipedia/CW221; page 15: © U.S. Federal Government; page 19: © Charles Daniel Howell; page 22: © Smontgom 65

Edited by: Luana Mitten

Cover and interior design by: Renee Brady

Library of Congress PCN Data

Condoleezza Rice / Precious McKenzie (Little World Biographies)
ISBN 978-1-62169-277-5 (hard cover)(alk. paper)
ISBN 978-1-62169-234-8 (soft cover)
ISBN 978-1-62169-416-8 (e-Book)
Library of Congress Control Number: 2012953418

Rourke Educational Media
Printed in the United States of America,
North Mankato, Minnesota

rourkeeducationalmedia.com

customerservice@rourkeeducationalmedia.com • PO Box 643328 Vero Beach, Florida 32964

Table of Contents

Growing Up in the South

How would you feel if you had bombs going off in your neighborhood? Condoleezza Rice grew up in Birmingham, Alabama, where there was **rioting** and **segregation**.

Black and white people were segregated in the South until the laws changed in 1964.

She saw **violence** happen in the 1960s. One of her kindergarten classmates was killed during a church bombing.

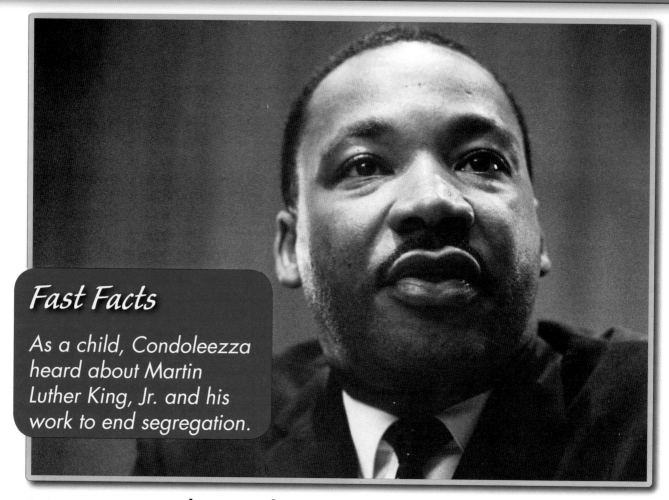

Fast Facts

As a child, Condoleezza heard about Martin Luther King, Jr. and his work to end segregation.

Many people spoke out against the unfair laws of segregation. Some people protested peacefully while others turned to violence.

Condoleezza's parents didn't want unfair racial laws to stop their daughter from doing great things with her life.

To Denver

Denver,
Colorado

Condoleezza and her family moved
to Denver, Colorado, when she was a
teenager. She loved to play the piano and
figure skate. She did very well in school.

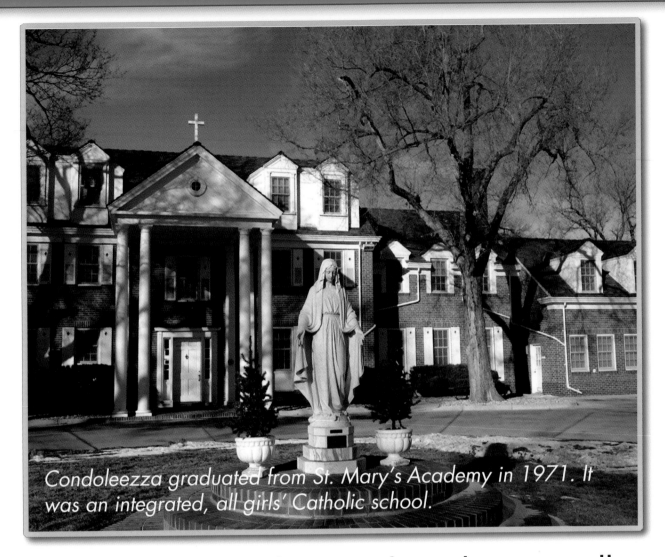

Condoleezza graduated from St. Mary's Academy in 1971. It was an integrated, all girls' Catholic school.

She took college classes when she was still in high school. Yet, a guidance counselor told her she wasn't college material.

Condoleezza planned to study piano in college. She changed her mind when she went to a **lecture** on political science. **Cold War** politics captured her interest.

Condoleezza graduated from college with highest honors at the age of 19 from the University of Denver.

Becoming a Professor

Condoleezza continued her college education. She went to graduate school to learn even more about political science. After Condoleezza finished graduate school, she became a professor at Stanford University.

Condoleezza won awards for excellence in teaching.

She wrote two books about the Soviet Union. Soon the president of the United States wanted Condoleezza to work for him. She worked on the National Security Council under President George H.W. Bush, directing America's affairs with the Soviet Union.

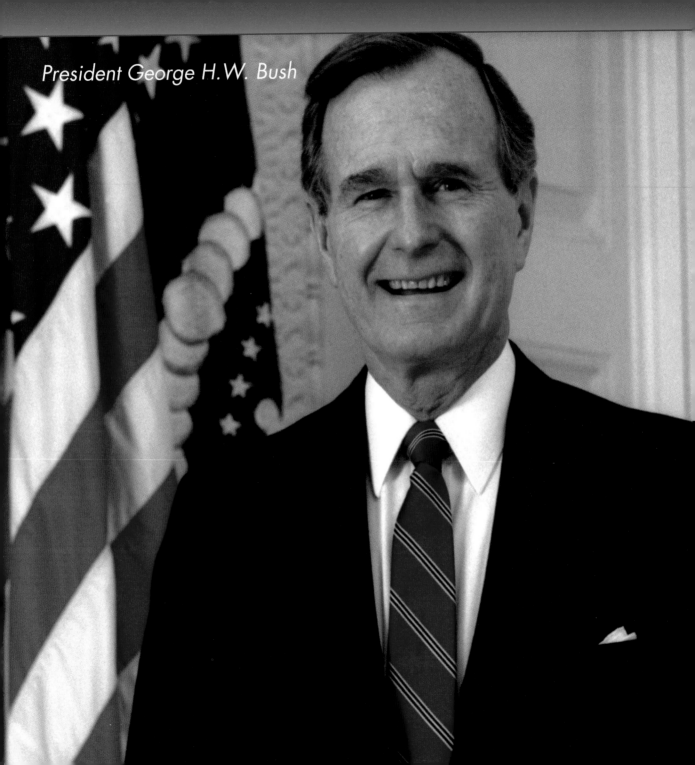

President George H. W. Bush

In 1993, she became the Provost of
Stanford. This was a huge milestone
because never before had there been a
black, female provost at the university.

Stanford University football coach Tyrone Willingham, and Stanford Provost Condoleezza Rice. Stanford University, 2000.

Condoleezza had to lead the university and keep track of its budget. It was a big job but Condoleezza liked challenges.

To Washington, D.C.

President George W. Bush with Condoleezza Rice.

In 2001, President George W. Bush named Condoleezza Rice as his national security advisor. She worked on foreign political strategy in the White House.

The World Trade Center during the September 11th attacks.

After the horrible attacks on September 11, 2001, Condoleezza Rice worked on new policies to deal with **terrorists**.

So Many Ideas

In 2005, Condoleezza became the Secretary of State. She was the first black female ever to have this role. She worked for peace in the Middle East. She also wanted to make sure countries used nuclear power for peace, not for war.

Although Condoleezza is no longer in office, she continues her work on human rights and safety. She has been called the most powerful woman in the world.

Condoleezza Rice speaks at universities across America. She wants to teach and inspire young people.

Timeline

1954	—	**Condoleezza born (November 14)**
1974	—	**Bachelor's degree from the University of Denver**
1975	—	**Master's degree from the University of Notre Dame**
1981	—	**Doctorate degree from the University of Denver**
1982	—	**Stanford University Professor**
1987	—	**Advisor to the Joint Chiefs of Staff**
1989	—	**Director of Soviet and East European Affairs on the National Security Council**
1993-99	—	**Provost of Stanford University**
2001	—	**National Security Advisor**
2005-09	—	**Secretary of State**
2012	—	**Spoke at Republican National Convention. Rumored to be a 2016 presidential candidate.**

Glossary

Cold War (KOHLD WOR): from 1945 to 1990, a time of extreme tension between the U.S. and the Soviet Union

lecture (LEK-chur): a talk given to a class or group

rioting (RYE-uht-ing): behaving in a very violent and chaotic way, usually destroying homes and businesses

segregation (se-gri-GAY-shun): separating people based on the color of their skin

terrorists (TER-ur-istss): people who use violence and threats to frighten others

violence (VYE-uh-luhnss): the use of force to do damage or harm

Index

Websites

www.kidzworld.com/article/3015-civil-rights-movement-timeline

www.whitehouse.gov/our-government

fun.familyeducation.com/black-history-month/holidays/32871.html

About the Author

Precious McKenzie lives in Billings, Montana, with her husband and three children. She loves to learn about American history and politics.

Ask The Author!
www.rem4students.com